The

Joy

Of

Martial

Arts

TOM SOTIS

ISBN # 978-1-7348045-5-3

Published by Thomas Sotis

tom@tomsotis.com
www.tomsotis.com

Dedicated to

Marina Trent

Acknowledgment

The credit for the value of the content and substance of this book belongs to the brilliant Prof Steven Reiss, the principles of which are organized and presented by the author through the lens of the martial arts.

Introduction

Early humans fought each other empty-handed, and they fought with sticks and stones.

Eventually we began fashioning weapons and developing hunting/fighting methods and techniques.

The evolution of fighting methods follows an unbroken thread woven through the history of mankind.

Since the dawn of humanity, our survival and the fighting arts are as intertwined as thirst and water.

It may be surprising to some that the martial arts, essential to our physical security, has evolved sufficiently to meet *all* our psychological needs as well.

Indeed, training in the martial arts can fulfill all of our deepest forms of happiness and contentment, which this book attempts to convey.

As you will discover, ultimately, we all share the same sixteen desires, but how we prioritize their importance varies, as does how much of those things we need to feel happy and content.

Individually, we find happiness and contentment in many forms but collectively, we all do it to satisfy the same basic desires.

The Joy of Martial Arts explains why martial artists pursue the martial way by revealing the unseen rewards that motivate us.

Let us proceed to A Template of Joy which tracks how and why we experience joy and its connection to our DNA-inspired survival instincts.

The sixteen joys that follow the template are presented in no particular order.

Sean Nel/Shutterstock.com

"The purpose of today's training is to defeat yesterday's understanding."
– Miyamoto Musashi

A Template of Joy

All humans share the same *needs*
each of which has a *goal*.

These creates our *desires*
in our pursuit of *happiness*.

Martial artists with a weak desire for
a goal tend to be *one-way* and those with
a strong desire tend to be the *opposite-way*
(note: average desires tend to be either-way).

Martial artists experience the
Joy of Satisfaction
when our desires are satisfied by getting
ideal amounts of the right activities which
stimulates a deep sense of happiness and
contentment.

Dani Llao Calvet/Shutterstock.com

"My opponent is my teacher; my ego is my enemy." - Unknown

Self-assurance

All humans share a need *not to commit suicide* the goal of which is *no criticism.*

This creates our desire for *acceptance* and our pursuit of *our own self.*

Martial artists with a weak desire for acceptance tend to be *confident* and those with a strong desire tend to be *insecure.*

Martial artists experience the

Joy of Self-assurance

when our desire for acceptance is fulfilled by receiving positive feedback from fellow trainees and teachers which stimulates a deep sense of happiness and contentment for, and within, ourselves.

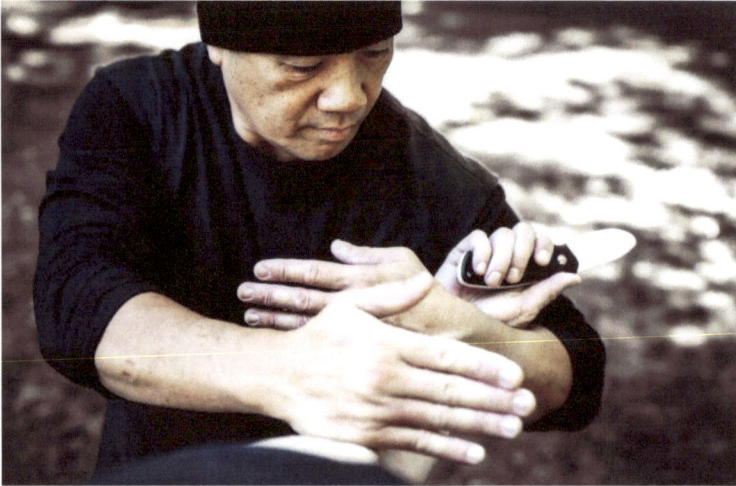

guruXOX/Shutterstock.com

"The true Martial Artist is a man so strong inside that he doesn't have a need to show his power." – Edmund Parker Sr.

Pleasantness

All humans share a need for *health*
the goal of which is *idyllic*.

This creates our desire for *beauty*
and our pursuit of *balance*.

Martial Artists with a weak desire for
beauty tend to be *suitable* and those with
a strong desire tend to be *attractive*.

Martial artists experience the

Joy of Pleasantness

when our desire for balance is fulfilled
by training environments which present the
ideal type of aesthetic satisfaction which
stimulates a deep sense of happiness and
contentment through *balance*.

"The Way of a Warrior is based on
humanity, love, and sincerity."
– Morihei Ueshiba

Wonder

All humans share a need to *learn* the goal of which is *thinking*.

This creates our desire for *curiosity* and our pursuit of *knowledge*.

Martial artists with a weak desire for curiosity tend to be *practical* and those with a strong desire tend to be *intellectual*.

Martial artists experience the

Joy of Wonder

when our desire for curiosity is fulfilled by activities which present the ideal amount of theory and practical application which stimulates a deep sense of happiness and contentment through *knowledge*.

Nomad_Soul/Shutterstock.com

"Put Karate into your everyday living; that is how you will see its true beauty."
- Gichin Funakoshi

Satiation

All humans share a *biological need*
the goal of which is *sustenance*.

This creates our desire for *eating*
and our pursuit of *refined taste*.

Martial artists with a weak desire for
eating tend to be *thin* and those with
a strong desire tend to be *overeaters*.

Martial artists experience the

Joy of Satiation

when our desire for eating is satisfied by
consuming the ideal amount of tasty food
which stimulates a deep sense of happiness
and contentment through *refined taste*.

"We must do whatever we can to aid the cause of peace of humankind and freedom and happiness." Masaaki Hatsumi

Love

All humans share a need to *perpetuate* the goal of which is *children*.

This creates our desire for *family* and our pursuit of *children*.

Martial Artists with a weak desire for family tend to be *not involved* and those with a strong desire tend to be *responsible*.

Martial artists experience the

Joy of Love

when our desire for family is fulfilled by sharing martial arts training and events with children and siblings which stimulates a deep sense of happiness and contentment through our *children*.

Nestor Rizhniak/Shutterstock.com

"To subdue an enemy without fighting is the highest skill." – Sun Tzu

Loyalty

All humans share a need for *support* the goal of which is *safety in numbers*.

This creates our desire for *honor* and our pursuit of *character*.

Martial Artists with a weak desire for honor tend to be *expedient* and those with a strong desire tend to be *trustworthy*.

Martial artists experience the

Joy of Loyalty

when our desire for honor is fulfilled by acts of brother/sisterhood between fellow trainees and teachers which stimulates a deep sense of happiness and contentment through *character*.

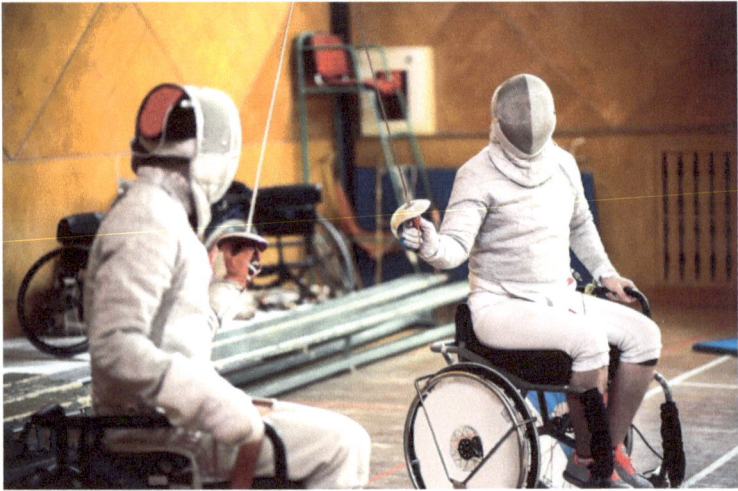

UfaBixPhoto/Shutterstock.com

"Limitations live only in our minds. But if we use our imaginations, our possibilities become limitless." – Jamie Paolinetti

Compassion

All humans share a need for *idealism*
the goal of which is *utopia*.

This creates our desire for *idealism*
and our pursuit of *social causes*.

Martial artists with a weak desire for
idealism tend to be *uninvolved* and those
with a strong desire tend to be *humanitarian*.

Martial artists experience the

Joy of Compassion

when our desire for idealism is fulfilled by
our group's stand on social issues and
community involvement which stimulates a
deep sense of happiness and contentment
through *social causes*.

Aleksandar Todorovic/Shutterstock.com

"I have repeatedly stressed that the ultimate goal of judo is to perfect the self and make a contribution to society". – Jigoro Kano

Freedom

All humans share a need to *find food*
the goal of which is *self-reliance*.

This creates our desire for *independence*
and our pursuit of *individuality*.

Martial artists with a weak desire for
individuality tend to be *dependent* and those
with a strong desire tend to be *self-reliant*.

Martial artists experience the

Joy of Freedom

when our desire for independence is fulfilled
by varied martial arts, schools, and
organizations which permit the ideal amount
of independence and *individuality*.

Ashwin pk/Shutterstock.com

"There is no comfort in the growth zone and no growth in the comfort zone."
- Unknown

Comfort

All humans share a need for *efficiency*
the goal of which is *structure*.

This creates our desire for *order*
and our pursuit of *stability*.

Martial artists with a weak desire for
order tend to be *disorganized* and those with
a strong desire tend to be *organized*.

Martial artists experience the

Joy of Comfort

when our desire for order is fulfilled
by arts and activities which present the ideal
amount of structure and organization which
stimulates a deep sense of happiness and
contentment through *stability*.

Oneinchpunch/Shutterstock.com

"A Black Belt is not something you wear;
it is something you become." - Unknown

Movement

All humans share a need for *physical activity* the goal of which is *movement*.

This creates our desire for *physical activity* and our pursuit of *fitness*.

Martial Artists with a weak desire for *physical activity* tend to be *inactive* and those with a strong desire tend to be *active*.

Martial artists experience the

Joy of Movement

when our desire for *physical activity* is fulfilled by workouts which present the ideal amount of exertion which stimulates a deep sense of happiness and contentment through *fitness*.

"The most dangerous person is the one who listens, thinks, and observes." – Bruce Lee

Achievement

All humans share a need for *dominance*
the goal of which is *influence*.

This creates our desire for *power*
and our pursuit of *competence*.

Martial artists with a weak desire for
power tend to be *laid-back* and those with
a strong desire tend to be *ambitious*.

Martial artists experience the

Joy of Achievement

when our desire for power is fulfilled by
learning a new skill, passing an examination,
winning a bout or competition, and many
other triumphs which stimulates a deep
sense of happiness and contentment through
competence.

Andy Gin/Shutterstock.com

"Sometimes people around you won't understand your journey. They don't need to; it is not for them." - Unknown

Preparedness

All humans share a need for *provisions*
the goal of which is *collecting*.

This creates our desire for *saving*
and our pursuit of *frugality*.

Martial artists with a weak desire for
saving tend to be *unprepared* and those with
a strong desire tend to be *prepared*.

Martial artists experience the

Joy of Preparedness

when our desire for saving is fulfilled
by collecting skills, certificates, belts,
awards, photographs and other memorabilia
which stimulates a deep sense of happiness
and contentment through *frugality*.

ildintorlak/Shutterstock.com

"Martial arts should be a way of life. Not a job, hobby, or sport but a part of you and the way you live your life." – Frank Gutting

Belonging

All humans share a need for *safety*
the goal of which is *companionship*.

This creates our desire for *social contact*
and our pursuit of *friends*.

Martial artists with a weak desire for
social contact tend to be *private* and those
with a strong desire tend to be *friendly*.

Martial artists experience the

Joy of Belonging

when our desire for social contact is fulfilled
by the friends we make at training which
stimulates a deep sense of happiness and
contentment through our *friends*.

PetrToman/Shutterstock.com

"A good instructor teaches you how to fight.
A great instructor teaches you how to live."
– Ricardo Almeida

Superiority

All humans share a need for *privilege* the goal of which is *standing*.

This creates our desire for *status* and our pursuit of *social class*.

Martial artists with a weak desire for status tend to be *informal* and those with a strong desire tend to be *formal*.

Martial artists experience the

Joy of Superiority

when our desire for status is fulfilled by receiving recognition and awards from fellow trainees and teachers which stimulates a deep sense of happiness and contentment through *social class*.

J. Henning Buchholz/Shutterstock.com

"If your mind is not projected into your hands, even ten thousand techniques will be useless." - Yamaoka Tesshū

Relaxation

All humans share a need to *flee-danger* the goal of which is *safety*.

This creates our desire for *tranquility* and our pursuit of *caution*.

Martial artists with a weak desire for tranquility tend to be *risk-takers* and those with a strong desire tend to be *cautious*.

Martial artists experience the

Joy of Relaxation

when our desire for tranquility is fulfilled by our martial activities which stimulates a deep sense of happiness and contentment through exercising *caution*.

girl-think-position/Shutterstock.com

"Conduct yourself in a manner that is worthy of respect and don't worry about what others think." - Bohdi Sanders

Vindication

All humans share a need for *self-defense* the goal of which is *getting even*.

This creates our desire for *vengeance* and our pursuit of *winning*.

Martial artists with a weak desire for vengeance tend to be *gentle* and those with a strong desire tend to be *brutal*.

Martial artists experience the joy of

Joy of Vindication

when our desire for vengeance is fulfilled by confronting those who offend us, and in matters of self-defense, which stimulates a deep sense of happiness and contentment through *winning*.

Dejan Dundjerski/Shutterstock.com

"If you are patient in a moment of anger you will escape 100 days of sorrow."
– Chinese Proverb

The Martial Way

As individuals we survive by meeting our physical and psychological needs, which we typically find easier to do in groups. As individuals, we seek to meet and sustain our individual personal needs within the culture of how our group operates to sustain itself.

We all share these same basic needs but the DNA-inspired strength of those individual desires varies, thus *creating polar opposite aspects of our personalities*, which naturally generates conflicts between people seeking to meet their varied individual needs in a group setting.

A paradox of existence is that we need each other to survive which forms the groups within which we conflict and, ironically, harm and kill each other.

The martial arts meet our basic need for self-defense and satisfies all of our most basic fundamental psychological drivers.

This accounts for why the martial arts are, to a greater or lesser extent, a universal activity in virtually every culture and why they bring so much joy and happiness to those who pursue the martial way.

About Prof. Steven Reiss

Steven Reiss, Ph.D. was the Founder of IDS Publishing Corporation.

He graduated from Dartmouth College, earned a Ph.D. in psychology at Yale University, and completed a clinical psychology internship at Harvard Medical School.

He was a Fellow of both the American Psychological Association and the American Association on Intellectual and Developmental Disabilities.

As a Professor of Psychology at the University of Illinois at Chicago and at The Ohio State University, he contributed original ideas, new assessment methods, and influential research studies to four topics in psychology: anxiety disorders, developmental disabilities, intrinsic motivation, and the psychology of religion.

His work developing Reiss Motivational Profiling® was recognized with five national awards for research, clinical services, and leadership.

About Tom Sotis

Tom Sotis has a unique background of life experiences that contribute to his excellence as a Trainer, Profiler, Coach, Writer, and Speaker.

Born in 1959, Tom is now well recognized as a pioneer and world leader in the fields of tactical combatives, personal safety, and as a high-performance coach.

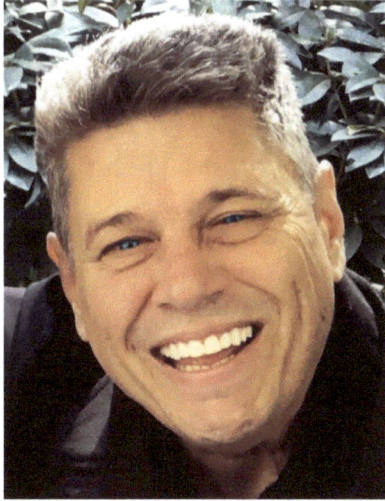

Having taught in 25 countries, Tom has earned world-renowned acclaim for his unique theories and coaching method.

For over 25 years, Tom has worked with US Intelligence Agencies, US Special Forces, US Secret Service, Federal Bureau of Investigation, and numerous other government agencies.

Tom became a certified Motivation Analyst licensed to administer and interpret the Reiss Motivation Profile®, *the world's first scientifically validated* and most accurate method of personality profiling and predicting behavior.

Today, Tom continues to enjoy traveling, training, coaching, researching, writing, and speaking. Please visit his website www.TomSotis.com to learn more about Tom:

Get your personal Reiss Motivation Profile®

This book introduces the principles of the Reiss Motivation Profile® and encourages readers to take the next step of getting their own personal profile.

The Reiss Motivation Profile® is a convenient online multiple-choice questionnaire that takes about 15 minutes and produces a one-page easy-to-read graphic, and a detailed report explaining your results (no jargon).

The test has potential of generating billions of outcomes which means no two profiles are the same and your personal profile will be as unique as your fingerprints!

You will have their report emailed directly to you and can opt for a personal online consultation with Tom so he may help you to better interpret its results, guide you to a more thorough understanding, and answer any questions you may have.

To get your profile please visit Tom's website www.TomSotis.com or contact Tom directly at tom@tomSotis.com

Tom's books are available on Amazon.com

The Way of Tactics: A Manifesto of Invincibility 2020

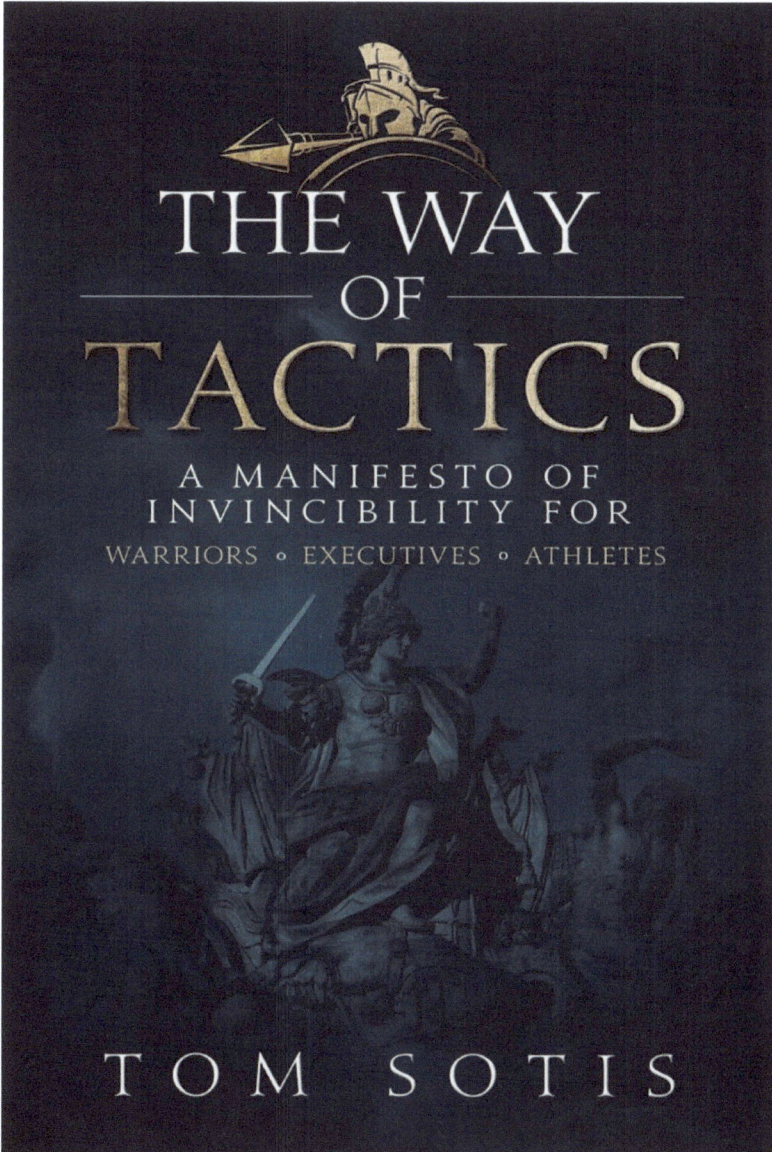

THE WAY

OF

TACTICS

A MANIFESTO OF
INVINCIBILITY FOR

WARRIORS • EXECUTIVES • ATHLETES

TOM SOTIS

www.ingramcontent.com/pod-product-compliance
Lightning Source LLC
Chambersburg PA
CBHW041816040426
42452CB00001B/1